TABLE OF CONTENTS

T0024428

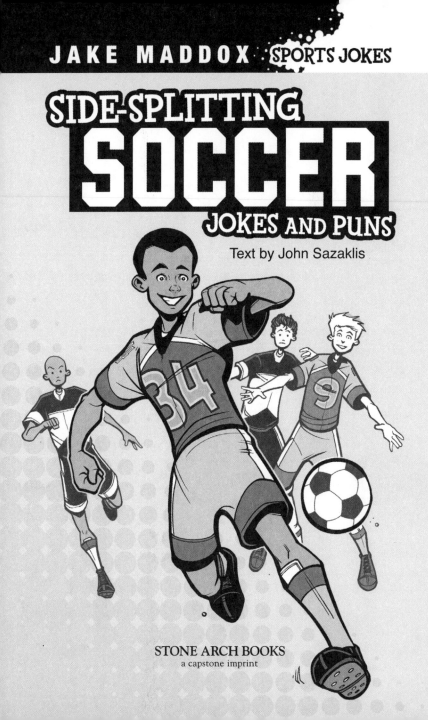

JAKE MADDOX SPORTS JOKES

SIDE-SPLITTING
SOCCER
JOKES AND PUNS

Text by John Sazaklis

STONE ARCH BOOKS
a capstone imprint

Published by Stone Arch Books, an imprint of Capstone.
1710 Roe Crest Drive
North Mankato, Minnesota 56003
capstonepub.com

Library of Congress Cataloging-in-Publication Data
is available on the Library of Congress website.
ISBN: 9781669074878 (library binding)
ISBN: 9781669074991 (paperback)
ISBN: 9781669075141 (ebook PDF)

Summary: If you love soccer—and a good laugh—then
this book is for you! With more than 180 rib-tickling
jokes, riddles, and puns, you and your friends will
be laughing out loud on every page!

Editor: Aaron Sautter
Designer: Jaime Willems
Production: Whitney Schaefer
Design Elements: Nana Chen,
Shutterstock/Vector FX

Printed and bound in China. PO 5827

SECTION 1:
ANIMAL ANTICS

Why don't grasshoppers watch soccer?

They prefer watching cricket instead.

What do you call a T-rex who kicks the ball into the net?

A dino-scorer!

Why shouldn't you play soccer in the jungle?

Because there are too many cheetahs!

What did the bumble bee forward say after getting a goal?

"Hive scored!"

How do birds cheer for their soccer teams?

They egg them on.

Why did the duck get ejected from the soccer game?

Because of all his fowl play.

Why didn't the dog want to play soccer?

He was a boxer.

What time is it when an elephant steps on your soccer ball?

Time to get a new ball!

How do you stop squirrels from playing soccer in your yard?

Hide the ball, it drives them nuts.

What soccer club do sheep like?

Baaaaa-rcelona!

Why do goats make good soccer players?

Because they head butt a lot.

Why can't you play soccer with pigs?

They hog the ball.

Did you hear about the coach who let his bloodhound play for his team?

It played scenter.

Why are dolphins good at soccer?

Because they dive a lot.

What do you get if you cross a soccer player and a mythical creature?

A centaur-forward.

What has 22 legs and is always chasing a ball?

A soccer team.

What is black and white and barks at the players?

The *ruff*-eree!

Why didn't the coach let the pigs play soccer?

Because they play dirty.

What do you call a team of monkeys that wins the World Cup?

The World *Chimp*-ions!

Why do dogs make terrible coaches?

Because they hound their players.

Why did the chicken cross the field?

To get to the other sideline.

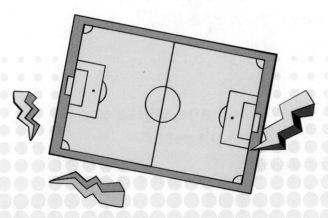

Why did the soccer ball quit the team?

It was tired of being kicked around.

Why does the soccer ball zoom around the field?

Because it gets a kick out of it.

Why couldn't anyone see the soccer ball?

The defense cleared it.

What did the soccer goalie say to the ball?

"Catch 'ya later!"

Why are soccer players good at starting conversations?

They know how to get the ball rolling.

Why can't Cinderella play soccer?

Because she always runs away from the ball.

What gets kicked all the time but never cries?

A soccer ball.

Where do soccer players dance?

At a soccer ball.

I didn't know where the ball went.

But then it hit me.

What do you call soccer player with fancy foot work?

A *ball*-erina.

What did the bratty player do when he lost the game?

He kicked up a fuss.

What did the soccer ball say to the forward?

I get a kick out of you.

What is black and white and red all over?

A soccer ball with a sun burn.

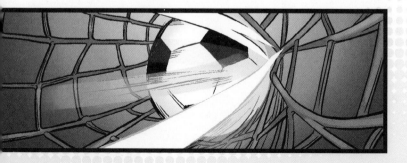

What should you do when you see a rhino with a soccer ball?

Get out of its way!

Why did the soccer ball go to the doctor?

Because it was feeling a bit deflated.

What did the goalie say to the ball when he caught it?

I glove you!

Did you know about the person who invented soccer?

They got a kick out of it.

What does a coach do when the pitch is flooded?

He brings in the subs.

Why did the coach give the soccer players lighters?

Because they lost all their matches.

Why did the soccer coach stand in the corner?

He wanted a time out.

Why did the angry coach break the referee's phone?

The ref made a bad call.

What walks back and forth screaming one minute, then sits down weeping uncontrollably the next?

A soccer coach.

What did the mummy coach say at the end of practice?

"Let's wrap this up!"

Why is the skeleton coach so calm during the game?

Because nothing gets under his skin.

What does the soccer coach drink at a cold game?

Hot penal-*tea!*

What's a soccer coach's favorite nut?

Pitch-stachio!

Did you hear about the coach who tried to quit soccer but couldn't?

He couldn't kick the habit!

Where does an old, retired soccer player go?

Out to *pass*-ture.

Why did the coach go to art class?

To draw up a winning strategy.

What do you call a soccer player who scores a lot of goals?

A *net*-worker.

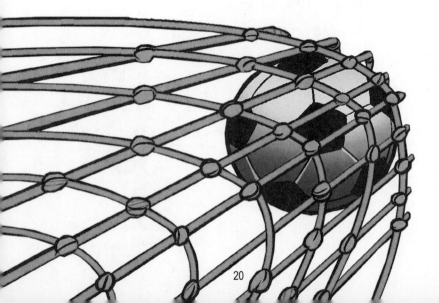

Why did the soccer player go to the bank?

To check his balance.

What do you call a boat full of polite soccer players?

A good sportsman-*ship*!

Why did the soccer player bring string to her game?

So she could tie the score.

Old soccer players don't die . . .

. . . they *pass* away.

When is a soccer player like a judge?

When he sits on the bench.

Which soccer player smells the nicest?

The "scenter!"

Why did everyone steer clear of the striker in the game?

Because he was pretty offensive.

What do a superstar soccer player and a magician have in common?

Both are great at hat tricks.

Why did the goalie propose to his girlfriend?

Because she was a keeper, too.

Did you hear about the soccer player who lived more than 100 years?

He's still alive and kicking.

What are the cheesiest soccer teams in the world?

Man*cheddar* United and Man*cheddar* City.

Why are scrambled eggs like a losing soccer team?

Because they've both been beaten.

Why couldn't the soccer team lose a goal?

Because the goal-keeper was too good at his job!

What time is it when a soccer team chases a baseball team?

Eleven after nine.

How did the soccer player break his bad habit?

He was able to kick it.

What's harder for a soccer player to catch the faster he runs?

His breath!

Have you heard about the soccer player who didn't clean his room?

He's a Messi guy.

Which goalie can jump higher than the goal post?

All of them. Goal posts can't jump!

What kind of soccer team cries after every match?

One with *"tear*-mendous" players!

Why did the losing soccer player use his hands?

He was tired of de-feet.

Seven days without playing soccer can make one weak.

SECTION 5:
WORLD CUP WACKINESS

What's the hardest thing for players in the World Cup?

The ground.

Why can't the World Cup star listen to music?

Because he broke all the records.

I got lost on the way to the stadium, so I stopped for directions. "How do you get to the World Cup?" I asked.

Do you know what they told me? "Lots of practice!"

What do you call a bunch of soccer fans in the basement after their team loses the World Cup?

A whine cellar.

How does the stadium stay cool during the World Cup?

Because there are so many fans.

Why is the stadium warmer after the World Cup?

Because all the fans have left.

Where is the World Cup held?

In the hands of the winners.

Which World Cup winner takes the goal home after the game?

The goal-keeper.

What did the bad World Cup announcer get for Christmas?

COOOOOOOALL!

Why is the World Cup such an unfocused game?

Because so many people are running away from their goals.

How did the ref know that the score would be 0–0 before the World Cup title game?

The score is always 0–0 before the game.

How do we Know that referees are having fun at the World Cup?

Because they whistle while they work.

Why should the World Cup end with an art class?

So it can be win, lose, or draw.

Why did the soccer fan toss his drink in the air?

He was celebrating a whirled cup.

What do soccer referees send during the holidays?

Red cards.

Why is fire safety important in soccer stadiums?

Because there are so many matches there.

How do soccer players listen to music?

On their 'header' phones.

Why was the soccer player such a bad dancer?

He had two left cleats.

Why can't people who wear glasses play soccer?

Because it's a *contact* sport.

Where's the best place to shop for a soccer uniform?

New Jersey.

Why do all soccer players wear shin guards?

Because they're very fa-*shin*-able!

Which soccer player has the biggest cleats?

The one with the biggest feet, of course!

Did you know that soccer players' socks have holes in them?

Of course, they do! How else would they get their feet in them?

Where do soccer players wash their cleats?

In running water.

When do soccer players wear suits of armor?

During knight games.

What did the soccer player do when he forgot his shin guards?

He kicked himself.

What's the difference between soccer shirts and soccer shorts?

One has an 'i' and the other has an 'o'.

Why is a soccer field great for musicians?

Because it has perfect pitch.

What runs around a soccer field but never moves?

The sideline.

Why was the soccer field wet on a sunny day?

The players dribbled all over it.

Which play is the sharpest in the game?

The corner kick.

Why are soccer fields so unsure about making decisions?

They have two opposing goals.

What do you call a woman standing between two soccer goal posts?

Annette.

Why was the clock kicked around the field?

The players wanted to pass the time.

Why are soccer practices always so noisy?

Because of all the drills.

What lights up a soccer field?

A soccer match.

Which soccer player keeps the field neat?

The sweeper.

SECTION 8:
KNOCK-KNOCK YOUR SOCKS OFF!

Knock, knock!
Who's there?

Wanda.
Wanda who?

Wanda play some soccer?

Knock, knock!
Who's there?

Dozen.
Dozen who?

**Dozen one know
the score?**

Knock, knock!
Who's there?

Lettuce.
Lettuce who?

**Lettuce win the
game, please!**

Knock, knock!
Who's there?

Olive.
Olive who?

Olive to play soccer.

Knock, knock!
Who's there?

Ice cream.
Ice cream who?

**Ice cream the loudest
for my team.**

Knock, knock!
Who's there?

You.
You who?

**Yoo-hoo, anybody
on the field?**

Knock, knock!
Who's there?

Radio.
Radio who?

**Radio not, the
game started!**

Knock, knock!
Who's there?

Venice.
Venice who?

Venice half-time?

Knock, knock!
Who's there?

A needle.
A needle who?

**A needle little help
with my soccer skills.**

Knock, knock!
Who's there?

Kenya.
Kenya who?

**Kenya blow the
whistle, ref?**

Knock, knock!
Who's there?

Boo.
Boo who?

Don't cry. We'll win next time.

Knock, knock!
Who's there?

Noah.
Noah who?

Noah place we can play soccer?

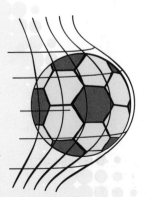

Knock, knock!
Who's there?

Adam.
Adam who?

Adam my way, I'm about to score!

Knock, knock!
Who's there?

Sue.
Sue who?

Sue-prize! We won!

Knock, knock!
Who's there?

Anita.
Anita who?

**Anita use the bathroom.
Call time out!**

Knock, knock!
Who's there?

Colleen.
Colleen who?

**Colleen up your cleats,
they're muddy!**

Knock, knock!
Who's there?

Annie.
Annie who?

Annie body got extra shin guards?

Knock, knock!
Who's there?

Candice.
Candice who?

Candice game get any worse?

Knock, knock!
Who's there?

Dewey.
Dewey who?

Dewey have to play in the rain?

Knock, knock!
Who's there?

Luke.
Luke who?

Luke for me so I can pass to you.

Knock, knock!
Who's there?

Orange.
Orange who?

Orange you going to shoot the ball?

Knock, knock!
Who's there?

Pudding.
Pudding who?

Pudding on your cleats before you play is a good idea.

Knock, Knock!
Who's there?

Alpaca.
Alpaca who?

Alpaca da uniforms and you pack-a da soccer balls.

Knock, Knock!
Who's there?

Toucan.
Toucan who?

Toucan play at this game!

Knock, Knock!
Who's there?

Goat.
Goat who?

Goat to the sidelines. You're benched!

Knock, knock!
Who's there?

A herd.
A herd who?

A herd you liked soccer. Let's play!

Knock, knock!
Who's there?

Weekend.
Weekend who?

Weekend win this game with teamwork!

Knock, knock!
Who's there?

Stopwatch.
Stopwatch who?

Stopwatch you're doing and let's play soccer.

Knock, Knock!
Who's there?

Witch.
Witch who?

**Witch one of you will
score the goal?**

Knock, Knock?
Who's there?

Woo.
Woo who?

**Why are you cheering?
We just lost the game!**

What position do ghosts play in soccer?

Ghoulie.

What do soccer players say on Halloween?

Hat Trick or Treat!

Why is the Invisible Man so good at soccer?

You never see him coming.

Why was the skeleton always left out in a soccer game?

Because he had no body to play with.

Why didn't the skeleton like to play soccer?

His heart just wasn't in it.

Why did the baby ghost join the soccer team?

They needed to boost their team spirit.

Who do zombies play soccer with?

Anyone they can dig up!

What's it like playing soccer with a vampire?

It's a real pain in the neck!

Why don't skeletons hurt when they head the ball?

Because they're boneheads.

What is a soccer player's favorite subject?

Geometry. Because they love making angles.

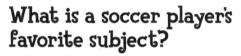

Why do soccer players do so well in school?

They really know how to use their heads!

What happens when a lazy defender takes a test?

He doesn't pass.

What are successful forwards always trying to do?

Reach their goals.

What kind of soccer club cries when it loses?

A bawl club.

Why did the soccer players go to ballet class?

To learn some fancy footwork for their game.

Why are soccer players the messiest eaters at lunch?

They can't use their hands.

Why are soccer players such good students?

They're always passing.

Why wasn't the nose on the school soccer team?

It didn't get picked!

Why did the soccer player stand on his desk?

So he could be at the top of his class.

Why are soccer players the quietest students?

Because silence is the *goal*-den rule.

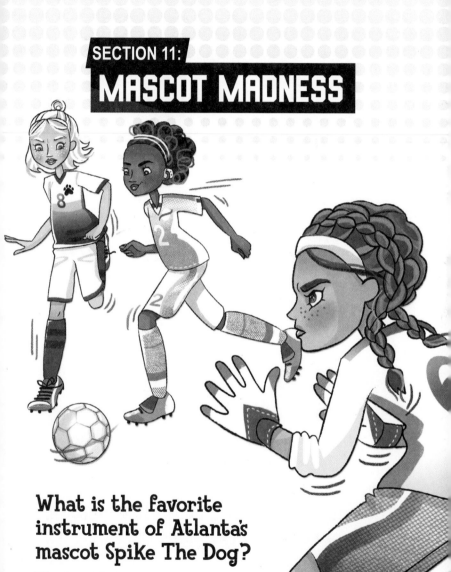

What is the favorite instrument of Atlanta's mascot Spike The Dog?

The trom-*bone*.

How can you find Sparky the Dalmatian at the Chicago game?

He's easy to spot!

Where does Orlando City's mascot, Kingston the Lion, work out?

At the jungle gym.

What do you call the FC Dallas mascot, Tex Hooper, when he's sleeping?

A bull-dozer!

Why does Kansas City's Blue the Dog stand in the shade?

So he's not a hot dog.

Why did Minnesota's mascot, PK the loon, fly south for the winter?

Because it was too far to walk.

What's the difference between a thunderstorm and FC Cincinnati's Gary the Lion when he's injured?

One pours with rain, the other roars with pain.

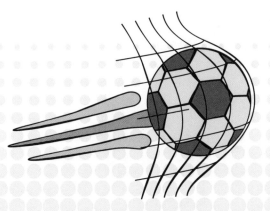

What do you call the Washington Spirit's mascot, PK the Eagle, when he teases the other team?

A mockingbird.

Which team's mascot has the freshest breath?

Sir Minty of Charlotte FC!

Why did the Montreal Impact's mascot Tac-Tik the dog chase his own tail?

To make ends meet.

Which instrument does Bulli from the NY Red Bulls play?

The cow bell, of course.

Why can't you trust anything Leo, Real Salt Lake's mascot, says?

Because he's always lion!

How does Utah's Cleo the Lioness keep calm during a game?

She keeps things in purr-spective.

What does the LA Galaxy say about their mascot Cozmo?

That he's out of this world!

Why did Colorado's Rapidman become a rapper?

Because he had some rapid flow.

What is Columbus Crew Cat's favorite dessert?

Mice cream.

How does New England's Slyde the Fox keep up with current events?

By watching Fox News.

Where does Seattle's Sammy the Sounder go when he's sick?

To the dock.

Did you know Nashville's Tempo the Coyote is also a comedian?

He's howl-arious!

Why is Philadelphia's Fang so famous?

He's in all the hiss-tory books.

Why did Chicago's Supernova become a mascot?

He wanted to make a big bang on the field.

What did Miami FC's mascot Golazo cheer when the team won?

"This is our lucky beak!"

Why is Tampa Bay's Pete the Pelican always working the crowd?

He's fishing for compliments.

Why did Reno's Truckee take a nap during the game?

Because he was *exhaust*-ed.

How does Richmond's mascot Kickeroo tell the team to get on the field?

"Hop to it!"

TELLING FUNNY JOKES!

1. Know your joke.

Be sure you memorize the whole joke before you tell it. Most of us have heard someone start a joke by saying, "Oh, this is SO funny . . ." But then they can't remember part of it. Or they forget the ending, which is the most important part of the joke—the punch line!

2. Speak up.

Don't mumble your words. And don't speak too fast or too slow. Just speak clearly. You don't have to use a strange voice or accent. (Unless that's part of the joke!)

3. Look at your audience.

Good eye contact with your listeners will grab and hold their attention.

4. Don't overthink things.

You don't need to use silly gestures to tell your joke, unless it helps sell the punch line. You can either sit or stand to tell your jokes. Make yourself comfortable. Remember, telling jokes is basically just talking to people to make them laugh.

5. Don't laugh at your own joke.

Sure, comedians sometimes crack up laughing while they're telling a story. And that can be pretty funny by itself. But normally, it's best not to laugh at your own jokes. If you do, you might lose the timing of your joke or mess it up. Let your audience do the laughing. Your job is to be the funny one.

6. Practice your setup.

The setup is the second most important part of a joke. This includes everything you say before getting to the punch line. Be as clear as you can so when you reach the punch line, it makes sense!

7. Get the punch line right.

The punch line is the most important part of the joke. It's the payoff to the main event. A good joke is best if you pause for a second or two before delivering the punch line. That tiny pause will make your audience pay attention, eager to hear what's coming next.

8. Practice, practice, practice.

Practice your routine until you know it by heart. You can also watch other comedians or a comedy show or film. Listen to other people tell a joke. Pay attention to what makes them funny. You can pick up skills by seeing how others get an audience laughing. With enough practice, you'll soon be a great comedian.

9. It's all about the timing.

Learn to get the timing right for the biggest impact. Waiting for the right time and giving that extra pause before the punch line can really zing an audience. But you should also know when NOT to tell a joke. You probably know when your friends like to hear something funny. But when around unfamiliar people, you need to "read the room" first. Are people having a good time? Or is it a more serious event? A joke is funniest when it's told in the right setting.

SOCCER TERMS TO KNOW

18-yard box (AY-teen YAHRD BOCKS)—the area near each goal that extends 18 yards to each side of the goal; also known as the "penalty area"

assist (uh-SIST)—a pass or other action that helps a teammate score

breakaway (BRAY-kuh-way)—when a player who has the ball gets past the other team's defense and rushes toward the goal

corner kick (KOHR-nuhr KIK)—a free kick from a corner of the field near an opposing team's goal

defenders (dih-FEN-duhrs)—players who are situated near their team's goal and contribute primarily to defense

fake (FAYK)—a quick movement, such as pretending to kick, pass, or dribble, designed to trick an opponent

forwards (FOHR-words)—players who play near the opponent's goal, focusing on offense

foul (FOWL)—an action that is against the rules

goalkeeper (GOHL-kee-puhr)—the player who defends the goal, also called the goalie

goal kick (GOHL KIK)—a free kick that is given to a defensive player when an opposing player drives the ball out of bounds over the end line

hat trick (HAT TRIK)—when a player scores at least three goals in a game

header (HED-uhr)—a shot or pass made by hitting the soccer ball with your head

kickoff (KIK-off)—the kick that starts play in a soccer game

midfielders (mihd-FEEL-duhrs)—players that normally play toward the middle of the field, contributing equally to offense and defense

offense (aw-FENSS)—the team, or part of a team, that is in control of the ball and is trying to score

offside (AWF-syd)—in a position on the opponent's side of the field where a player isn't supposed to be during a game

penalty kick (PEN-uhl-tee KIK)—a free kick at the goal, granted because of fouls or other violations that occur near the goal

scrimmage (SKRIM-ij)—a practice game between members of the same team

throw-in (THROH-in)—a throw made from a player on the sideline to put the ball back in play

tournament (TUR-nuh-muhnt)—a series of matches between several players or teams, ending in one winner

trap (TRAP)—to stop and gain control

ABOUT THE AUTHOR

John Sazaklis is a New York Times bestselling author of more than 100 children's books! He has also illustrated Spider-Man books, created toys for *MAD magazine*, and written for the BEN 10 animated series. John lives in New York City with his wonderful wife and dynamic daughter.

READ THEM ALL!